Bourgeois Poetry

by

Vicki Roberts

Bourgeois Poetry by Vicki Roberts

ISBN 978-1-63110-424-4

For information:

Vicki Roberts, Esq.

vicki@RestMyCase.com

To my husband,
Arthur Andelson,
My true inspiration

Table of Contents

Page

Bourgeois Poetry

Conjoined

We are joined at the hip through no choice of our own,
Separating our bodies is not presently known;
We cannot go to vent in our own separate rooms,
When undoubtedly we clash and an argument looms;

When one of us feels, the other one follows;
An unwilling witness to joy and to sorrows;
We don't know privacy in any sense at all,
Not even for the hope of a lover's call;

The days and the nights are all closely aligned,
We each do our bidding confined by our bind;
Our blood lines entwined through organs and limbs,
We used to be known as Siamese twins;

A true friend for life, a sister from birth,
We cherish our gift to be part of this earth;
We laugh and we smile and we engage all of life,
Our happiness thrives in spite of our strife;

Yet when one of us suffers, the other must pray,
The malady to pass to live another day;
In sickness and health 'til death us do part,
Wedding vows for most but it's the matter at heart;

It started out tame with a simple cough,
We truly believed in a day it would off;
With each struggled breath, each gasp was the worst,
It seemed so hard her lungs just might burst;

Then news arrived from the powers that be,
There is no cure, no magic key;
Suddenly I found myself tethered to a bed,
My sister a shell, my fears turned to dread;

The cold truth upon me, no time to reflect,
Is there still a pulse, I checked and I checked;
Unchain me, oh Lord, my sweet heaven now hell,
I don't want it to ring, that eulogy bell;

She died twenty minutes ago on the clock,
My time is shrinking by tick and by tock;
My hourglass empties some time in this night,
I'm not sure what's worse - the fate or the fright;

The evening approaches, time never sits still,
Yet I am robbed of my own free will;
My sister is cold, she's rigid and white,
Our vows never broken, I join her tonight.

The Prisoner In The Hoosegow

Oh what a tyrant this prisoner be,
Everyone knew of his awful crime spree;
Ghoulish attacks were the tools of his trade,
Carving his victims with a serrated blade;

What did possess this criminal mind,
Newspapers scoured his past so to find,
Where did he inherit such horrible worth,
Not much was known, just adopted at birth;

The pony express brought news of his cause,
Townsfolk were eager to avenge broken laws;
Pioneers traveled from all the frontier,
Hungry to witness the trial of the year;

One by one they countered his plea,
Victims who lived said why yes, it is he;
I'll never forget that face oh so clear,
Never did I witness or have me such fear;

The jury convicted with nary a fight,
All in the room were united in right;
Guilty as charged, as the gavel went down,
Justice was served, a relief to the town;

Year after year the monster would dwell,
Pacing and rotting in his singular cell;
Always maintaining his clear innocence,
Not a soul could he manage to ever convince;

One day a crime of a similar bent,
Frightened the crowd wherever they went;
The public had long since forgotten the soul
They condemned to serve time in a hellish black hole;

The face of this villain eerily bore
The countenance of the one we convicted before;
Suddenly the shock rippled through the vast land,
It cannot be the one we forever banned;

The criminal laughed as they held him at bay,
It was I, you fools, your blame you mislay;
Ne'er did I know I've a brother, a twin,
You gave him the credit for my evil sin;

Robbed of his years, far from freedom's gate,
A good man was doomed by a twist of fate;
Where does one go to retrieve time long lost,
No payment to make for this terrible cost.

Toy Soldier

He was just a little boy who spoke not a word,
He'd point or he'd grunt if he wanted to be heard,
He had a toy soldier which was his best friend,
They always played army, though it was only pretend;

He taught his toy soldier to aim and to shoot,
The soldier understood even though they were mute,
His toy ammunition was loaded in place,
The weapons were ready, the soldier kept pace;

The adults were content to allow him his time,
No playmates came by, no matter, no crime;
He had his toy soldier to groom and to train,
It took away the loneliness, a misfit's pain;

His soldier was old, bore the Union Jack,
In revolutionary times he'd be praised to attack;
The colonists betrayed their fealty vow,
This is not something a loyalist could allow;

At night when the child was tucked in for bed,
He placed the toy soldier in his toy shed;
And dreamt through the night as he tossed and he turned,
Content with his student and all he had learned;

The house doors were locked, the neighborhood tensed,
A strange spate of killings had nightly commenced;
The sniper was sharp in his deadly reign,
He moved through the streets in a quest inhumane;

Boston was cold this time of year,
The townsfolk were frozen, by weather, by fear;
Who would be safe, who would be spared?
None ventured out, not one soul dared;

The boy lay awake with a yawn and a grin,
Morning had come, time for play to begin;
His soldier was there, at the ready to serve,
With starched uniform, with spirit and verve;

He reached for his comrade, his daily retrieve,
But this time he noticed red specks on its sleeve,
He brought it to mother to show her the spray;
She gasped as she grabbed the toy soldier away;

The mystery solved, matching blood on the site;
His toy soldier had come alive in the night;
To avenge his brethren from the heathens in town,
Who sought to defy and sully the crown;

The little boy mourned, his lone friend destroyed;
No one to play with or to fill in the void;
How could this be, he panicked and fret;
He started to cry and his brow broke a sweat;

Suddenly awakened by this nightmare and fright;
The boy sat up in bed and turned on the light;
His toy soldier sat steely, with nary a peep,
He sighed in relief and went back to sleep.

Antietam

It was the bloodbath battle of the Civil War;
Scores of men died, by musket, the gore;
Was this brave dead soldier from north or from south,
Left on the field, blood gushed from his mouth;

He had a young sweetheart, love oozed from her breast,
But he never came home, just like the rest;
Was he union or confederate, his uniform too soaked;
His features so mangled his loyalty cloaked;

His flesh turned rancid as decay set in,
The maggots rejoiced in the bounty of sin;
Some looters took aim at his lockets and gear,
Never mind that his kinfolk would hold them so dear;

The generals conferred in their well armed tents,
In their starched uniforms acting oh so like gents;
Was it a victory or was it a draw?
No one was sure, the loss was too raw.

The bloodiest day in the land's history,
It turned the war's corner, that's no mystery;
But at the end of it all only one thing is sure:
Dead is dead, and for that there's no cure.

The Weaver's Rumination

Spin, spin, spin, 'round the massive loom,
Peddle that treadle, watch a pattern bloom;
No time for rest, pay is by yard,
Never have I worked this long or this hard;

The sweat on my brow drips into my eyes,
It burns as I squint, my will it defies,
The shop is so humid there's no air to breathe,
Yet onward I press, more fabric to weave;

The thread never ends, the skein of yarn calls,
The drudgery wears on within these four walls;
A laborer's wage is all I will earn,
Like butter I melt as this contraption I churn;

At the end of my shift I am spent beyond thought,
My back is so stiff and my fingers too taut;
And as I collapse on my bed for to sleep,
I know that tomorrow the same work I keep;

My tapestry masterpiece displays on the wall,
Adorning a palace, admired by all;
No one who sees it gives pause to my grind,
I'm the most distant thing from anyone's mind;

Yet there in that grand salon of repute,
Hangs my beautiful work, there is no dispute,
My artistry captured forever in place,
My existence confirmed, 'tis my saving grace.

The Lonely Cowpoke

He's up before dawn to get out the hay,
Horses need feedin' no matter the day;
Check out the gates, fastened and locked,
No room for rustlers, make sure they're blocked;

Slop for the pigs, grain for the hens,
Work dawn to dusk, no time for friends;
Roosters are squawking to awaken the sheep,
The barn is untidy, in need of a sweep;

Where are the buckets to hand milk the dames,
He hadn't a sweetheart but knew the cows' names;
Nanny goats roam as billies make chase,
Better hurry up, ladies, and quicken the pace;

The donkey brays for its mate down the field,
He watches their coupling, their future is sealed;
Llamas snuggle close as their wool intertwines,
Caws of wild birds making love on the vines;

One day a delivery came to the gate,
Supplies to replenish, but a happening of fate;
The merchant took ill, sent his filly instead,
Her golden mane flowed and dizzied his head;

Before long a smile formed beneath his mustache,
His ardor was stirred, it arose in a flash;
He chewed his straw grass as he pondered his move,
Calm and serene, he had nothing to prove;

He pinched off a daisy and offered his prize,
She accepted the gift with lust in her eyes;
His spurs tossed aside as they dropped to the floor,
And the lonely cowpoke was lonely no more.

The Handyman's Lament

So many tools to play with all day,
Where shall I start, there's work every which way,
Wrenches and hammers and C-clamps galore,
Lathes and tile saws and oh so much more!

The wife's in the kitchen with pastries she bakes,
Sweet pies and cookies and all kinds of cakes;
But my toys are not there, they're in my garage;
And I just can't resist my tools to massage;

I have gadgets, devices, contraptions to use,
Does anyone know a better way to amuse?
I'm sure there is something in need of repair;
I need an excuse to be in my lair;

Where is my drill, I know it is here,
I thought I put it right next to my beer;
The tape measure's here, so are the screws,
But if I find that damn drill, now that'll be news;

There are boxes and bins with all kinds of scrounge,
So many projects, no time to lounge;
But it's getting late, time to call it a night,
My handyman dreams about to take flight;

So goodnight my pliers, my nails, and my bits,
My level, my box cutter, and of course my vice grips;
I'll see you tomorrow at dawn's early light,
Until then my sweet babies, I bid you good night.

The Train

Each week at the station I'm set to depart,
On the same journey, to meet my sweetheart;
So many faces who share the same ride,
Some with their papers behind which they hide;

There's Harry the hatter repairing a cap,
And a squinting cartographer drawing a map,
Then there's the guy who adds and subtracts,
Dripping with sweat as the total impacts;

That young girl commutes to the city school,
Her backpack reveals a purple slide rule;
The woman behind her is rapt in a book,
How to make food, perhaps she's a cook;

We go round and round on the circular track,
Pass the same places and then we go back;
Everyone sits in the very same seat,
They don't seem to move, I can't see their feet;

The train lights then flash and the whistle blows,
The ride is over, that's how it goes;
We come to a stop but nobody moves,
The train cars remain in their rutted grooves;

The lights go off and the children take leave,
Playtime is over, it's late in the eve,
I'm left at the depot, a tiny toy swain,
Waiting to board my favorite toy train.

The Demagogue

Ladies and gents, I'm here to assist,
But let's be clear, it's futile to resist;
Pie in the sky, I give you your turn,
Never mind the details, they're of no concern;

To the people I give hope, in them there's the power,
There have to be changes I shout from my tower;
The crowd roars in glee as they wave their placards,
Little do they know as they let down their guards;

There's strength in their numbers, these feeble-minded masses,
They needn't know I think they're uneducated asses;
Easy to placate and easy to con,
Give me some time and their freedom is gone;

It's time for the vote, my denizens in place,
To make sure the outcome is clear in this race;
Commandeer the ballots and secure the right count,
Hurry it up lest the fears start to mount;

The results are in and my victory secure,
The media confirm that the outcome is pure;
Now to begin my grooming of youth,
Make sure the books don't tell them the truth;

Take away their guns, their lines of defense,
Give them a reason that doesn't make sense;
Call out the objectors, shame them on end,
'Til there is nothing left to defend;

Who is this traitor within elite ranks,
Off with his head, no more from the flanks;
My command is infinite, no room for slack,
All is well, I needn't watch my back;

I didn't see it coming, these bands of dissent,
With dogged grit these wretches hell bent;
My palace is burning, my army retreats,
I dismiss as weak their blood curdling bleats;

They've breached the wall, the courtyard is filled,
Most of my men have fled or been killed;
Oh no I feel something below my left eye,
A sharp-shooter's piercing, to make sure I die;

My strength is weakening, my limbs have gone numb;
I hear the faint beat of a different drum;
I'm fading from life as my reign disappears,
Off in the distance the populace cheers;

Goodbye sweet world, I called you my own,
My ego consumed, I've been overthrown,
I squandered my chance to do right and do well,
My fate is now sealed, as I travel to hell.

The history oft writes of itself never more,
Not to repeat the lessons of yore;
A warning to one and to all be aware,
Lest the next demagogue brings his tidings to bear.

Keep your means of defense and your freedoms held
dear,
The march of the despots is ever so near;
Vigilance rewards the free and the brave,
Make sure to guard it from cradle to grave.

Money Woes

I love my yachts, my cars, and my house,
Not sure why I'm considered a louse;
I pick up the tab when we dine on the town,
Yet their disdain for me is hard to pin down;

I know that humility is not my strong suit,
Why should it matter, they partake of my loot;
I'm the first one they call for tickets to games,
But the last one they want to hang out with the dames;

They use me, abuse me, so shallow their goals,
Nothing runs deep, seem so empty their souls,
They are pretty people, they make me look good,
I'd like to have more, if only I could;

But wait just a minute, how then should it be,
I'd really like someone who liked me for me;
That girl at the shop seemed authentic and all,
Maybe I'll chance it and give her a call;

Her face lightened up whenever I passed,
I never considered to regard such a lass;
A pang of discovery suddenly arose,
Priorities bungled, that's how I chose;

I swiftly discarded my list of non-friends,
Pages and pages without dividends;
Tossed in the shredder, ne'er to look back,
No need to recall my character's lack;

Will she still have me, the girl I ignored,
Have I what it takes to be her adored?
I'll try something new, my soul to expose,
Forget the riches, try one single rose;

Well after a while of courting my love,
My wishes granted from the Lord up above;
I'm thankful I had my flash of good sense,
A heart filled with riches I now can commence.

The Hurting

My young son is sick, his illness unknown,
I will never give up, she was quick to bemoan;
As he lay dying, the sick child so pale,
Her anguish profound, her little one so frail;

What an angel is she to sacrifice so,
Long suffering woman, wrapped in her woe;
What can we do to help you, my dear,
The neighborhood joined in their offers sincere;

They brought her supplies with their sympathies deep,
They checked on her daily, a vigil to keep,
Try as they might the doctors perplexed,
Each one in sequence a little more vexed;

By sheer will she endured as she soldiered on,
A mother's love for her son, her grit never gone;
Strong as she controlled the medicine drip,
She wrested him nightly from the Grim Reaper's grip;

What is this wicked illness so rare,
We cannot determine, it's so awfully unfair;
Yet just when it seems he is doomed to succumb,
He retunes his mien to a healthy life's strum;

Take your medicine, my son, finish your drink,
Again he is stricken as he's brought to the brink;
Help me, my friends, I'm drowning in grief,
My baby is suffering, I need some relief!

What could account for one's trust so defiled,
A mother's need to abuse her own child?
Is it wicked, deranged, or lunacy's touch,
All that we know is what's known is not much;

Help me, my son, he's so terribly ill,
Affliction controlled alone by my will;
Munchausen by proxy is a daunting name,
Twisted love, a most dangerous game.

The Food Addict

A delicious omelette with butter and toast,
How could I resist what I love the most;
On to the bagels with cream cheese and lox;
After which I'm raiding the cookie box;

Only hours 'til lunch I am planning my haul,
Shall it be deli or fish, I'd rather eat all;
Then there's my nosh later on in the day,
Don't block the kitchen, get out of my way!

For dinner I'll start with a big bowl of soup,
Potato pudding's divine, ok, just a scoop;
The red meat is rare, the juices do flow,
But once again I'm eyeing that cookie dough;

To top it all off I'll have the sorbet,
It's the beginning of the end of my food bingeing day;
Right before bed there's that last bit of cake,
With my tummy so full, I can't stay awake;

Food is my lover, it coddles my pain,
It's my one drug of choice, my potent cocaine;
I love how it tastes on my palate so fine,
It shows me no mercy, I just can't decline;

Maybe one day the source will reveal,
Why I attack it with such fervor and zeal;
But for the moment I have much to do,
There's French toast to make and coffee to brew.

The Narcissist

I am the one who rules the roost,
This is the unmitigated truth;
No one will know my hidden torment,
Low self esteem from my tortured youth;

Challenge my will and teach you I will,
They'll all think it's you and not me;
Threaten my world in my perceived way,
Shame and contempt surely yours is to be;

My lies are truth, 'tis the edict I charge,
My word is the golden goose,
Defy me and learn the fate that awaits,
For you it's the trap door's noose;

You refuse my rules, you ungrateful beast,
Now I must gather my troops,
And spin fiction and yarns of your errant acts,
To divide and conquer the groups;

They suckle my milk as it pours from my breast,
As I assign to you faults that are mine;
The minions are rapt by the tales that I've pressed,
Hanging gladly on every course line;

Oh what an ecstasy this feeling brings,
A scapegoat to have all my own,
A constant fuel for my starving self love,
As I wriggle in delight and I moan;

I'm sure it is you who offended me so,
I'm adrift in my unending wrath,
Yet nothing I say will ever be the same,
The wind has a more certain path;

My bane is your bane - projection's my game,
But somehow my audience wanes,
No one indulges my whim or my claim,
They care not for my hurt or my pains;

The clock ticks and tocks with relentless glee,
And suddenly everyone's flown,
The flock has dispersed and tired of me,
Now I'm here by myself all alone;

When I was young my worth went unheard,
Try as I might I was shunned-not a word;
I did have value, I wish I had known,
Now I am here by myself all alone.

Cocoon Comfort: Ode to Solitude

Oh how I love the comfort of home,
Room to room I wander and roam.
No one to see me undressed to the nines,
No one to hear my grumbling and whines.

Where I do shuffle on old worn out socks,
Where I don't answer when somebody knocks;
There where I most want to stay and to play,
There where I piddle about in the day.

Ne'er past the threshold beyond my front door,
Why leave my cocoon? Please tell me what for;
'Tis easier to wallow in the warmth of my bed,
'Tis funner to snuggle with Chaucer, nuff said.

Would that I had but a friend now and then,
We could prattle and jabber and clack in the den,
But that would require my zest and my ken;
And I'd really prefer just my paper and pen.

So here as I lay me in bed way past two,
My cur by my side, her wet nose dripping goo,
I rejoice in my choice to remain out of sight,
Please just leave me alone for to groan and to write;

For whatever is said at the end of my time,
The least they could say is I managed to rhyme;
And for what it is worth I never did bore,
With a plethora of words I just couldn't ignore.

Now it's time for my closing, my lids they do droop,
The body is fading, it goes as a group;
Tomorrow is here, it has come way too soon,
Hark, another day shines in my cocoon.

To My Dear Husband

When we first met I wasn't so sure;
I needed a kiss on the way out the door,
To sample the flavor and savor the taste,
Lest not my heart be subject to waste.

The sweet nights were many, the lonely ones few,
'Tho we relished and rowed as lovers often do;
Still something did draw us to cling well as one,
The love that was kindling would not be undone.

We surged and we ebbed in the dance of the game;
The joy and the thrill; the dark, the mundane;
The silence, the chatter, the murmurs of night,
We honored our troth from the day of our rite;

The years have marched on as we age and we wither,
Yet ne'er did I question, or teeter or dither;
And with the swift passing of all of our days,
My heart bursts alive in so many ways.

So thank you, dear husband, for love and for joy,
Since for some my poor soul was only a toy,
I share with you me, 'tis all I possess,
And when we're no more, our souls to caress.

The Meddler

She walks like the wind
All in a flutter,
With her head in the air
And her nose to the gutter.

Like a heat seeking missile
With her slitlike eyes,
She threads her needle
Of gossip and lies.

There's no freedom to be,
There's always a spat,
An unrelenting nag,
Don't do this, don't do that.

Too much time, too much space,
She's all in your hair,
Her maw is her cudgel,
She brings trouble to bear.

What sayeth the horde,
The enablers of old?
We beseech thee to wrest
The crone from her hold.

But the crowd doth protest
Too much: not enough;
The food at her trough
Is too sweet to rebuff.

So on goes the meddler
Secure in her reign,
By all those who coddle
Her words of disdain.

But beware all ye kinfolk,
Beware all ye fools:
The meddler maintains
An arsenal of tools.

No one is safe,
No one's secure;
She's a meddler my friend:
She is nothing more.

Ode to My Friend Raquel

My dearest Raquel with your terrible cough,
What will it take for this habit to off?
Blackened lungs, scarred and tarred, cry out for relief,
There still is some time to turn over that leaf,

With life oh so precious, then poof it is gone,
More songs to be written, why make it your swan,
The birds will still fly, their youngsters delight,
How wondrous it is to watch their first flight;

Far be it for me to say from my perch,
That which you know from church or from search,
I only wish goodness and toast to your health,
To continue to marvel in all of earth's wealth.

We all get subsumed, no one is spared,
Whether we're ready or not well prepared,
No need to rush toward the ultimate end,
There are still many paths to meander and wend;

Choices are hard, commitments can be worse,
Especially with matters claimed as a curse;
Best wishes to you and all those you love,
I wish you courage from within and above.

The Laundry Slacker

So, it's piled high and deep and it's reeking of sweat,
Both old clothes and new ones and some that are wet;
There is way too much here for a single load,
This means I'm stuck now in laundry mode;

I'm running low on soap and there's grime on the floor,
Much I'd prefer to walk out the door;
But it won't wash itself so get started I must,
Do this work first and then off to dust;

Though before I start on my list of to-dos,
I just want to finish up reading the news,
With a hot cup of java to sip while I read,
And maybe some toast, to sate hunger's need;

That went too quickly, alas I am done,
Better pull the knob and let the water run,
Just a sec while I check on my mail,
Unanswered missives have gotten so stale;

Don't call me lazy, I just take my time,
What is the rush, there's no pressing crime;
That pile is still calling, it never lets up,
I guess I should start, it's soon time for sup;

In with the powder and on with the switch,
It won't wash itself, ain't that a bitch,
Stalling's divine, it's never a chore,
Now I'm back at the pile with one dishrag more.

After the wash there's the dry and the fold,
Today it's the hot, tomorrow the cold;
A myriad of socks missing their mates;
Still I linger as the hamper awaits;

There's just that one article I wanted to read,
And a refill is needed on the wild birds' seed;
I just remembered there's a recipe to bake,
I'm a slacker indeed, make no mistake.

Now as I lay me down to my sleep,
Soiled togs forsaken and ready to weep;
I didn't quite finish the one task at hand,
Ah, truth, a slacker's goals never go as planned.

Ode To Hurricane Dorian

With a thunder and roar like a hungry beast,
It whirled and it whipped as it readied its feast,
Its course full of fury with nary a mind,
It lashed and it thrashed as it drank and it dined;

No one to save and no one to spare,
All in its track ought be wise and beware;
The scorned woman pales to its unquenchable wrath,
And all kings bow to its chosen path;

The strong and the weak are equal at last,
No power is greater or nearly as vast;
It knows not of wealth nor position of right,
All are as one, whether meek or of might;

This dangerous beauty is alone in its ire,
Its tantrum a rage that ne'er seems to tire;
Yet after its reckless life doth expire,
Its wondrous existence is heaped on the pyre;

For no matter the destruction and what it has wrecked,
This exquisite soul demands our respect,
What a staggering and stunning truth of this earth,
To remind us how much or how little our worth.

The Bemused Muse of Poetry

Some will be light and some will be frothy,
Some will be deep and complex;
Reactions of glee and of joy may be plenty,
Others may pout and may vex;

Comments and grumbling fill the great room,
Nothing will stop her: we are destined to doom;
With eyes rolled skyward, the crowd gasped in fear,
On seated edge they waited to hear;

Oh, there she goes, again and again,
Spewing her rhymes like an old worn out hen;
When does it end, her quest ne'er to sate,
All she does is exasperate!

Opinions may shift and undoubtedly vary,
Some will move on, others will tarry,
Still she marches to her singular tune,
Searching and seeking her next thought to prune.

The day closes down, the night doth appear,
The lids start to dim, bedtime is near,
What colorful dreams await and beguile,
The morrow's gifts shall appear in a while.

Just One More Verse

Where are my glasses, my shoes and my cane,
I'm sure they're around, where were they last lain;
Where was I going and what did I say,
Does anyone know the week or the day?

Facts from past decades are here in a snap,
I can even find Prussia on an old wrinkled map;
But your question ten minutes ago is just lost,
I guess that's the reality of old age's cost;

Rainbows of experience color my dreams,
I'm never an invalid there so it seems;
Wouldn't trade any of it again to be young,
Not even when told my swan song is sung;

I want to leave my mark to show I was here,
For those who are strangers and those I hold dear,
Not sure the calendar day of my fate,
Etched in my tombstone that second date;

I do know I'm near to the end of my time,
No more to speak or to write or to rhyme,
Better hurry up and finish this verse,
If you're still reading I beat out the hearse.

The Roseate Spoonbill

The roseate spoonbill skims the lagoon
Then wades in the shallows by light of high noon;
She knows not of troubles both past and to come,
She lives in the moment, be it wild or humdrum;

What beauty has nature created so grand,
One who takes flight over majestic land;
Then alights gracefully at water's edge,
Yawing her bill as she sifts through the sedge;

And when the night falls she finds a thick shrub,
Avoiding the gators who seek her for grub;
Her body kept warm by her feathery quills,
She sleeps undisturbed in her nest with no frills;

Then up at dawn the cycle renews,
Another wet habitat for fishing to choose,
With focused purpose to fill up her craw,
Oblivious to her own magnificent awe;

Wouldn't it be nice to emulate her ways,
Never to worry about tomorrow's frays;
No bills to pay, no papers to file,
Just fish for food and rest for a while;

No need for comforts of home or acclaim,
Riches mean nothing, survival's the game;
A peaceful world filled with nothing indeed,
Nothing but life and just what we need.

When I Was Famous

When I was famous they clamored for more,
Each one jostled to get in the door,
For a glimpse of my countenance and a chance for a pic,
A brief conversation, but please make it quick;

My time is more valuable than yours'll ever be,
I've another red carpet, I'm hot can't you see;
I get a preferred table at Michael's grille,
They're so thrilled I'm there they cover my bill;

Never mind you wait while I sashay my way,
Ahead of the line while you're kept roped at bay;
Fawning and worshiping my every word,
The sycophants drool, tho' the matter absurd;

Free tickets to shows and swag suites galore,
Pose with my product, oh what a bore;
But do it I must, the minions I game,
The limelight shines bright as they gorge on my fame;

A new crop of starlets has come on the scene,
Clawing the audience away from my sheen;
Suddenly I'm brushed aside by the paps,
No longer asking for interviews or snaps;

A trip to the market is eerily muted,
It's stunning to me how my star is diluted;
It's over, there's nary a soul in my sight,
I'm left writing poetry alone in the night.

www.ingramcontent.com/pod-product-compliance
Lightning Source LLC
LaVergne TN
LVHW041209080426
835508LV00008B/876